D1180807

pond features & decorations

pond features & decorations

Philip Swindells

Interpet Publishing

Published by Interpet Publishing,
Vincent Lane, Dorking,
Surrey RH4 3YX, England

ISBN 1-903098-38-6

Editor: Philip de Ste. Croix
Designer: Philip Clucas MSIAD
Studio photography: Neil Sutherland
Production management: Consortium,
    Poslingford, Suffolk
Print production: Leefung-Asco Printers
    Trading Ltd, China
Printed and bound in China

THE AUTHOR

Philip Swindells is a water gardening specialist with a
long experience of growing aquatic plants in many
parts of the world. He trained at the University of
Cambridge Botanic Garden and the famous aquatic
nursery of Perrys of Enfield, and ultimately became
Curator of Harlow Carr Botanical Gardens, Harrogate.
The author of many publications on water gardening,
Philip was also formerly the editor of the *Water Garden
Journal* of the International Waterlily Society who in
1994 inducted him into their Hall of Fame. He was
awarded a Mary Hellier Scholarship in 1990 by the
International Plant Propagator's Society for pioneering
work on the propagation of waterlilies.

Acknowledgements
The publishers would like to thank the
following people and companies for their much
appreciated help and advice during the
preparation of this book: 'G' at Old Barn
Nurseries, Dial Post, Horsham; Hillhout Ltd for
providing decking timber and a bridge for
photography; Murrells Nursery, Pulborough,
West Sussex; and Stuart Thraves at Blagdon,
Bridgwater, Somerset.

contents

introduction

The water garden is generally regarded as a natural setting which essentially depends upon plants, fish and a balanced eco-system for success. This is unquestionably true, but there are many additions and improvements that can be made which can make it visually more appealing. Whether it be a bridge that permits the scene to be viewed from a different angle or lighting which extends enjoyment into the evening, the opportunities for adding extra pleasure and value to the pond should be thoroughly explored.

A water garden can be greatly enhanced by transforming it from being merely a static pond or rambling stream into a more integrated part of the garden landscape. Stepping stones are both functional and decorative and they also change the flow and sound of the water, while a cobble beach banked up at the edge of a pond provides a convincing link to the surrounding garden, as well as a place of easy access to the water for birds and other wildlife.

Bridges and causeways offer additional ways of seeing the water, as well as the practical means of passing from one side of a feature to the other. Decking provides the perfect setting for relaxation and enjoyment of the watery scene. Pond edging is another area where decorative and functional issues coincide. Do not look at the point where the pond meets the garden as a problem area; view it

instead as an opportunity. Timber, paving stones, grass and coir rolls can all be integrated into the water garden and provide a satisfying way of linking the pool to its surroundings.

Lighting is probably the most important addition that a water gardener can make to enhance enjoyment of the pond. Modern lighting is simple to install and available in a wide range of configurations that offer opportunities for gardens of every size. Provided that instructions are followed properly, such installations are completely safe and can transform the most modest water feature into a glittering nighttime experience. Lights are available that go in the pond to uplight fountains and other features, or for the poolside to throw light behind or beneath plants and statuary.

Great possibilities are offered by wet and dry islands which enable the gardener to establish a small, self-contained growing environment in the middle of an expanse of water. Planted rafts, as well as other floating features, also provide interesting ways to create interaction between hard landscaping features and the fluidity of water. With such marvellous options available, all imaginative water gardeners should look seriously at the many ways in which they can further enhance what is arguably the most attractive feature in the garden.

Above: Garden lighting can transform a water feature after dark.
Right: While water and aquatic plants are the main component of a water garden, much can be gained by introducing additional features. A bridge provides the opportunity to enjoy the pond from a different viewpoint.

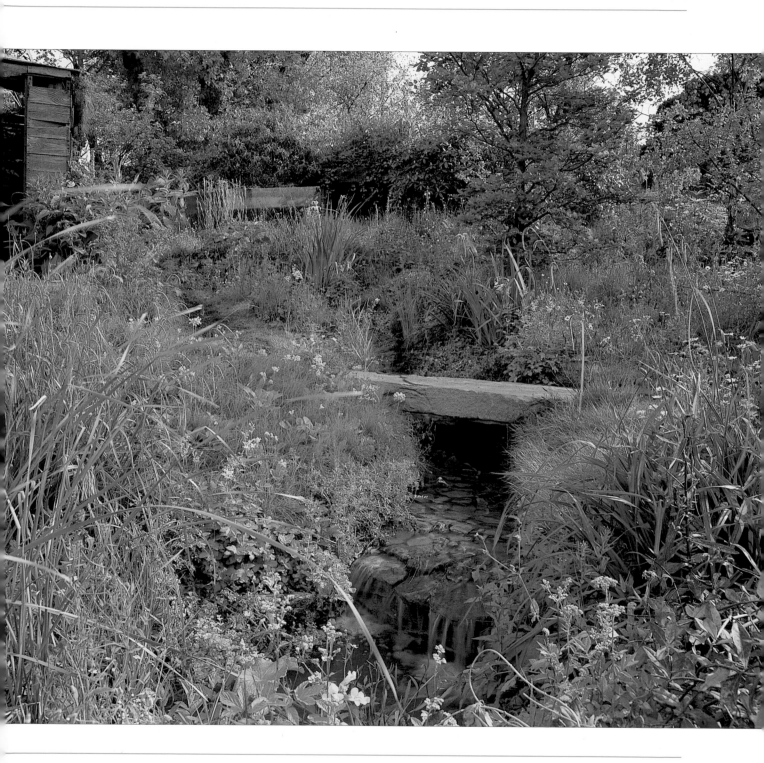

decking

Decking is an extremely popular landscape material. Pioneered in the United States, in recent year it has taken Europe by storm. Most decking is of high quality timber, but there are synthetic and often recycled materials also available. Originally timber decking was offered as a rustic means of achieving various objectives with walkways, causeways and sitting-out areas, but now it has become fashionable to paint it in all manner of interesting 'designer' shades.

Right: *The extensive use of decking here not only provides a neat edge to the poolside – it has become an important part of the water feature in its own right. The timber harmonizes with the water, and offers an area for poolside recreation without detracting from the importance of the pool itself.*

Left: *A combination of natural materials – the informality of the stones and gravel contrasts with the formality of the beautifully shaped decking. Timber is a very versatile edging material, conveniently disguising what lies beneath.*

Lower right: *Apart from providing a neat solution to edging a water feature, decking can also provide access, as here by means of a causeway. If carefully planned, the structure can contribute positively to the ambience of the water feature.*

From the point of view of the water gardener, when decking is suitable visually, it can provide the most useful and functional of pond edging. Not only is it a first-class disguise to conceal the ugly edge of a pond, but, when properly and sturdily constructed, it is an ideal place from which to survey and enjoy one's watery endeavours.

Decking can also be used to great effect as a causeway across a large expanse of water, or as a landing stage or a similar extension into the pool allowing the water to be appreciated from a different viewpoint.

Although rarely treated as a background for plantings, when handled in this manner decking can be extremely effective, especially for surrounding and isolating individual plant specimens. This applies both in the water with taller marginal subjects as well as on drier land where soil conditions are more regular and stately architectural plants, like bamboos and rheums, flourish. Such plants are wonderful for the backdrop of a water garden and their foliage can soften the angular harshness of some traditional decking and assist in uniting the water feature with the rest of the garden.

lighting

It seems improbable that electrical lighting should be associated with water, but in fact it can be a harmonious partner. Not only does it highlight plants or objects located on the bank, but it can also be used within the pond as well. Modern garden lights of suitable manufacture can be placed almost anywhere within or around the pond – submerged lights being particularly effective.

Of course electricity and water can be dangerous bedfellows, but modern wiring circuits using transformers and low-voltage cables ensure that there is no danger of personal electrocution, nor of decimating the fish population. Providing that all the manufacturer's instructions are followed, there is no reason why pond and garden lighting cannot become a permanent, safe and most enjoyable feature of the garden landscape.

While most garden lighting draws on the electricity from the house or garage, increasingly solar energy is coming to the fore as a power source. How well this performs depends largely upon where you live and how much sunlight your garden receives, although some manufacturers have developed a system whereby recharging takes place even in cloudy conditions so lights can operate almost whatever the weather.

Below: Underwater and external lighting can transform a pond in the evening, creating a magical effect with shadows and reflections.

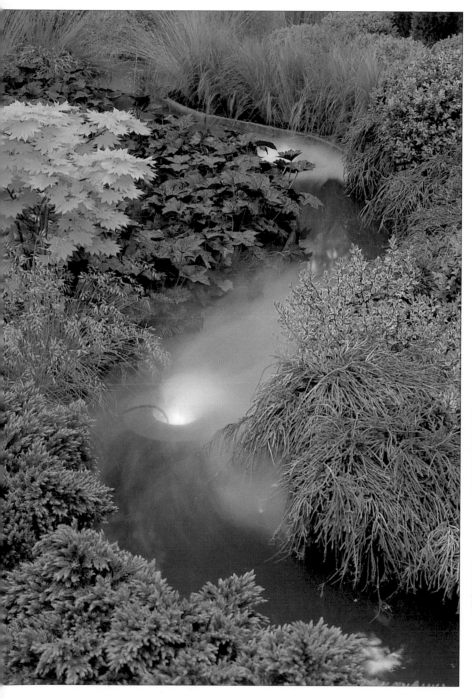

However, for the best and most reliable light, electricity is to be preferred. It is bright and consistent. Apart from highlighting static features, it can be used to uplight fountain sprays, not only with white light, but also with an array of contrasting colours when used with tinted lenses. These need not be static colours, for it is possible to attach a rotating disc containing several different lenses beneath a fountain jet to produce a rainbow of delight.

Left: Lighting can be used to highlight the rushing and tumbling of water. When combined with a fogger unit, turbulent rapids become an atmospheric river of fire.

Above: The most spectacular use of lighting is with a decorative fountain feature. Carefully placed uplighting can bring a touch of grandeur to a small water garden.

stepping stones

The best way to cross a shallow band of water is by walking on stepping stones. Not only are they visually appealing and easily installed, but they are great fun, especially for children. It almost seems as if you are walking on water.

Stepping stones can also be used to divert the flow of water in a stream. Their presence can narrow the channel or push the water in varying directions, so effectively increasing or decreasing the flow. Apart from the visual effect that this may have, the turbulence created also changes the sound of moving water.

Stepping stones were originally natural stones that were placed in the water at strategic points to enable passage from one bank to another. Any flat-topped stones were used. This is still the most attractive and natural method of creating a crossing, although from a safety point of view each stone should have a level upper surface and be able to generously accommodate a large foot.

Choosing natural stones carefully is important – many of those derived from sandstone or limestone are so soft that they shale and disintegrate when exposed to very cold temperatures in water. The surface should also have a grip so that there is no danger of slipping; some of the granites and millstone grits are excellent in this respect.

Nowadays garden centres are full of different kinds of manufactured stepping stones made from both concrete and reconstituted stone. They are all excellent; the only decision to make is the choice of the shape, texture or colour that suits you best.

Below: *Stepping stones enable the garden visitor to traverse the water and also to view the pond from a different perspective. Although functional, stepping stones should also ideally be decorative.*

Above: *Stepping stones and paving can be used in a variety of configurations and associations with a water garden. They provide a means of crossing the water, but they also compartmentalize it and so become an integral part of the design. The use of the urn as a highlight to lift the eye, together with the careful positioning of plants with varying leaf forms, add much to this arrangement.*

Left: *The placement of stepping stones need not be conventional. Their arrangement in diamond shapes and multiple groups makes a refreshing change and provides an excellent complement to the adjacent parterre hedging.*

13

bridges and causeways

Where there is a stream, rill or other ribbon of water in a garden, there is a natural desire to bridge it so that it can be viewed from another angle. There is also something entrancing about standing above water and viewing it from an overhead perspective. Bridges have long been the means of doing this, although across more open stretches of water or boggy ground raised causeways may be used.

Some bridges are very simple and it is their lack of an elaborate structure which gives them their charm. A plain length of stone or a single plank of timber can be functional in enabling you to cross a tiny rill or stream, but they also add visual appeal to the garden scene. Likewise the traditional clapper bridge with its minimal support enchants the eye by its simplicity.

Bridges in a garden rarely exist solely as a functional means to cross water. Indeed, in some cases water is an excuse to build a bridge which is intended to become an

Below: A highly decorative bridge is the focal point of this garden. The glassy stillness of the water allows for pleasing reflections.

Above: A causeway permits the enjoyment of waterlilies and other aquatic plants at close quarters. In addition, it provides easy access for maintenance and contributes positively to the overall aquascape.

important focal point or garden feature. Some specially manufactured bridges are as intricate, expensive and elaborate as the most desirable pergola or summer house. These are often manufactured like furniture and sold in flat-packs for on-site assembly. More elaborate and expensive creations tend to come ready-made to place in position and they are best installed by a contractor.

Of course bridges do not have to be prefabricated. Although the majority of those seen in the home garden will be of such manufacture, DIY construction from stone or brick is a further option, but not one for the novice or faint-hearted handyman.

floating features

Provided that they are suitably tethered, there are a number of floating features which can add much to the appearance of a water garden. The most impressive is the floating island. Islands are really only successful when surrounded by a reasonable expanse of water. Most aquatic enthusiasts concede that a pond measuring less than 4.5 x 4.5 metres (15 x 15ft) is unsuitable as an island will tend to crowd it out.

This is particularly so with a floating island as it is usually constructed from a standard wooden pallet. Strategically positioned empty plastic drinks bottles give the raft-like structure buoyancy and compost packages can be incorporated between the slats for planting. Such an island has to be anchored to the floor of the pond and sufficient length of rope or chain attached beneath to allow for fluctuating water levels. In a gentle breeze the raft moves around – as it may drift to the limits of its rope tether, unless the open water area it occupies is substantial, the effect can look foolish and out of keeping.

Other satisfying floating features include lights that float just at or slightly beneath the surface of the water. These are wonderful for creating up-lit effects upon objects or plantings in and around the pool. They are available in a wide range of colours, but it is traditional white light that produces the most striking effects.

When the weather is appropriate, or for the indoor pool, floating candles are fun. Still conditions are desirable for their stability and to ensure a sparkling, flickering flame. Other fun effects can be created by coloured balls that float across the water's surface, submerged sculptures that give a *trompe l'oeil* effect of a floating form, or even the drift across the pool of mist that is created by submerged 'foggers' – small electrical devices that use sound waves to atomize water and so create artificial fog.

Below: The modern gardener has a wide array of floating objects available for use in the contemporary pool. Currently decorative balls of various colours are in vogue.

Left: Even something as simple as a floating decoy duck can bring an extra touch of interest to a garden pool. When used in conjunction with floating plants and profuse marginal and pondside planting, the effect is very pleasing.

Below: Although not strictly floating, this clever portrayal of the character Bottom from Shakespeare's A Midsummer Night's Dream deceives the eye into believing that the head is swimming in the water. Such ornaments are unexpected and fascinating for both children and adults alike. They benefit greatly from being planted around with deep-water aquatics like waterlilies which have floating leaves and blossoms.

islands

Islands generally look out of place in a small pond, for they also have to be small. Thus they lose much of their meaning and *raison d'être*. In addition a small island is much more difficult to construct than one of reasonable dimensions. Occasionally pre-formed pools offer an apology for an island in their design. Rarely are these of any great beauty, even when appropriately planted.

Even when an island is visually appropriate to a pond, its function is often not primarily a decorative one, but rather it is intended to provide a predator-free sanctuary for

Right: *Islands look best visually when surrounded by sufficient water. In most water gardens, a well-planted island such as this looks completely natural but in reality it is contrived. Where a tree or shrubs can be included, this is a great advantage, especially for the dull winter months. Here an oriental feel is conveyed by the beautifully shaped pine tree, although the peripheral plantings are in the western tradition.*

Left: *When it comes to a formal pool, an artificial island is much more in keeping. Square or circular islands which reflect the shape of the pond are most pleasing to the eye. These can also be used for some highly coloured planting, especially when built as a dry islands where bedding plants can be used.*

wildlife. Such an island can usually be satisfactorily accommodated in a pond with minimum dimensions of 4.5 x 4.5 metres (15 x 15ft).

The construction of islands, although wide and varied in method and material, is best carried out after the pond has been created. Unless the pond is to be a natural earth-bottomed structure sealed with bentonite clay, then much better control over the island structure can be achieved if it is added afterwards.

In a pond erosion of the island's margins is a potential problem and construction has to take this into account, while at the same time striving for as natural an appearance as possible. Few islands are appealing unless

Below right: *A contrast in styles – the peacefulness of the grass islands set off by their silver surrounds and the glassy stillness of the water is challenged by the riotous red planting in the borders and urns behind. These are built as dry islands isolated from the pond.*

planted, so suitable provision must be made for successful establishment of a variety of plants. Although an island is surrounded by water, it is possible to isolate it from this influence by the use of liner or brick walls in order to create dry conditions on the island itself. So, while the planting of 'wet' islands in most cases will consist of appropriately marginal or bog garden plants, if the soil within is separated from the water by a liner, summer bedding may be more appropriate in a 'dry' island.

edging with stone

The most difficult element to get right is the pond edge. Doing it correctly can certainly make the feature, while getting it wrong will ruin it completely. Whether the pond is formal or informal, the edging used is ultimately a matter of personal choice. It is certainly more usual to use paving stones for a formal feature and a stone-led planted edge for an informal one, but there are no unbreakable rules. Materials should be used that suit personal tastes and practical circumstances.

Edging is quite clearly visible and defines the pool. Wherever possible it should overhang slightly in order to protect the liner when a pond is of this construction. It should also be arranged to disguise the ungainly plastic or fibreglass edge of a pre-formed pond. The other important

Below: Stones and cobbles are among the most satisfactory of edges for a natural pool. Awkward edges can be easily disguised, and the use of stones as a beach is of benefit to bathing birds and wildlife.

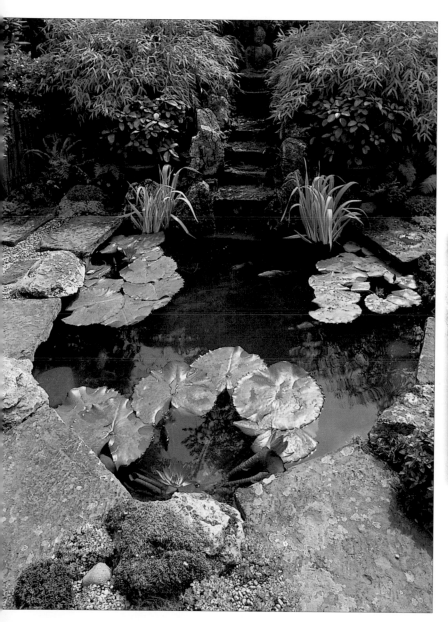

consideration is to make the edge very stable, especially if it is an area which will be walked upon.

Where stones are used as opposed to regular paving, they should be selected not only for their beauty, but also for their resistance to extreme weather. This is especially important if they come in contact with the water, for many sandstones and some limestones shale or crumble when they are saturated with water and then frozen in winter.

Although real stone is always deemed to be most desirable, nowadays there are very convincing reconstituted stone products that are easier to use. Not only are they of uniform or consistently variable shape and size, but also of a stable structure. Thus when having to cut them to fit particular circumstances, there is little chance of them splitting and shaling in unexpected directions. Natural stones often exhibit very tiresome weaknesses when it comes to cutting them.

Above: *When using stone slabs, ensure that there is an overhang at the pond edge. This disguises the area where pond meets garden and reduces the effect of sunlight on an otherwise exposed liner.*

Above right: *The use of large stones to create the effect of a mountain pool works well when there is sufficient space for bold planting. This pool combines modern pavers with ancient rocks.*

edging with timber

Timber is a natural edging, but is not always one that fits best with a natural pond, for its most common use is in providing good secure straight edges to formal features where it can be easily fastened with screws or bolts. Properly treated timber used in this fashion is inexpensive and quite long-lasting, although it does not have the durability of stone.

Raw timber with its bark intact is often used to great effect out of the water in those areas where a bog or marsh garden is being established. Here it provides an informal and natural surround for the bog garden or for pockets of

Below: Timber can be used in a variety of ways in the water garden, from simple edging to providing a surround to a hot tub, as seen here.

planting which extend out from the pond. It is unsuitable for use beneath the water, but will serve as a water garden edging for many years, often developing its own colonies of saprophytic fungi and other interesting wild flora.

Log roll is also a useful edging, especially in a formal situation. Extensively used in many guises in the garden from path edging to creating a raised bed, it is especially effective when used both to edge the pond and to create marginal planting areas lower down in the water. Consisting of short lengths of prepared and treated round or half-round timber fastened with galvanized wire, log roll

Above: *Provided that it is properly treated, timber can be used extensively in the water garden, both to edge a pond and as the main structural material, as is the case with these linked raised pools created from sleepers. It is best employed in formal situations and is one of the easiest materials for the practical home gardener to use.*

has great flexibility of form and is capable of being arranged in both simple formal, as well as complex informal, configurations. A similar effect can be achieved with the use of short lengths of large-diameter bamboo drilled and bound with tarred rope. This creates a very special oriental effect.

natural edging with plants

While timber and stone unquestionably provide the widest range of opportunities for creating imaginative pool edging, there are other methods which are visually appealing and often more appropriate.

One of the simplest and most effective is the raised beach. Primarily used for providing access for wildlife to more natural water features, it can be used most effectively in a formal situation, especially when carefully selected cobbles of uniform colour are used in association with grass or planted margins.

Grass edging is also appropriate for all kinds of ponds. It can produce a clear-cut straight edge for a formal pond or tumble over the edge into an informal feature. However, it is not without its problems when it comes to maintenance, for it is important that grass cuttings do not enter the water where they will decompose. Happily, this is not impossible to control and the resultant contrast between grass and water is worth the little extra effort that is necessary to care for the edges regularly.

Planted edges are also important, although many gardeners do not regard plants as edging as such. This is a pity because the correct choice of plants with all the right functional qualities, which at the same time are pleasing to the eye and appropriate at the waterside, can create the most effective edging of all. They should be mat-forming species and varieties of tumbling growth, ideally evergreen or partly so and with an ability to prosper in moist soil but at the same time not resent occasional inundation. The archetypal plant of this type is brooklime, *Veronica beccabunga.*

Below: *Plants are particularly convincing when planted amongst poolside stones and rocks. The beautifully tended lawn running to the water's edge creates a wonderful effect.*

Left: *Plants can be used freely for edging a pond provided that the water depths are compatible. With natural plantings in an earth-bottomed pond, the edges can be defined by soil sculpting – the plants only advance as far as the water depth permits.*

Below: *Strong plantings of a single variety such as irises are essential to create a bold effect for large open spaces of water. Well-planned soil sculpting before planting will confine the irises to the desired area and their tightly knit roots will form an erosion-proof edge to the water feature.*

ornaments and decorations

The opportunities for using ornaments in a water garden are legion. Nowadays there is an industry in manufacturing everything from classical nymphs or water carriers to specially toughened mirrors or stainless steel abstract sculptures.

Beauty is in the eye of the beholder, but sometimes one has to question some of the weird timber, steel and glass creations that are installed in modern water gardens. Provided that the pond is clear-cut and formal, such flights of the imagination can work, but for the majority of gardeners designs of a more classical nature still tend to be preferred.

Ornaments used in water gardening are often associated with the movement of water, either as items in which fountains are incorporated or linked with cascades or chutes. Often this is the best way to enjoy ornaments in a water garden setting, especially if they can be enhanced by lighting.

Ornaments should not be afterthoughts. Just as the planting has to be considered carefully in order to create an overall balance, allowing for various depths and zones, so the introduction of an ornament should also be considered carefully from the outset, especially with regard to its placement.

Unlike ornaments that are used in beds, borders or as focal points in the main garden, there is another aspect to consider when decorative objects are used in or beside water. Water in all its moods and reflectiveness can have a profound effect upon the visual character of an ornament. Whenever possible, take into account the ever-changing nature of water itself when planning how you may introduce an ornament into your waterscape.

Right: *There are countless opportunities for the use of ornaments and decorations with a water garden. Here a wide combination of decorative effects is exploited, from the ornamentation within the structure of the mosaic pond itself to associated watery artefacts like shells and starfish, and the use of mirrors which give the impression of being windows to a garden beyond the blue wall. Water clarity is of vital importance here but it will be impossible to achieve by natural means. Water changes will be needed to keep such a feature looking good all year round.*

Left: *Straight lines and clearly defined angles emphasize the simplicity of this modern water feature. Uncluttered by planting, it makes a strong statement which is highlighted by the sinuous sculpture. Decoration need not be fussy – equally pleasing effects can be achieved by a single well-placed piece like this, which provides a striking focal point.*

making your own decking

As decking has become increasingly popular, it is now quite easy to purchase timber suitable for decking projects from local timber merchants or garden centres. While decking used to employ standard timber treated with a wood preservative, nowadays it is available in an array of specially manufactured configurations, usually tanalized to make it weatherproof. The deckboards are made with longitudinally grooved surfaces which are not only non-slip, but also visually appealing.

When it comes to making your own decking, the first and most important consideration is to purchase the best quality timber that you can afford. Cheap timber sparingly treated with preservative not only looks poor, but will have a very limited life.

It is vital to ensure that all supports for decking are substantial; timber uprights should be at least 10cm (4in) square and either set in concrete or dropped into a metal fencing sleeve or pipes set into concrete. The maximum distance between structural posts should be 180cm (6ft). The boards themselves are mostly 15cm (6in) wide, although it is possible to get both narrower and wider deckboards. The gap between boards when they are fastened to the subframe should be no more than 5mm (0.2in); make sure that whatever gap you leave is consistent across the whole deck. The space permits the timber to move in different weather conditions and lets rainwater drain away freely. Remember to treat any sawn ends with a proprietary sealer to make them weatherproof.

Decking screws are now widely available and are the best method of securing the timbers to their supports, although there is still a place for bolts, especially where strong uprights require connecting. Alternatively galvanized deck ties can be used to secure boards to the joists. The successful construction of decking depends upon careful planning and accurate measurements. But with some forward planning, it is not as complex a task as it may at first appear.

CONSTRUCTING A DECKING PLATFORM

1 *The timber framework for decking should be substantial and the individual bearers placed at intervals to provide good support. These should be set no more than 45cm (18in) apart, but ideally 30cm (12in), especially over water.*

2 *Having ensured that the framework is square and tightly secured, the first deckboard is placed in position at the desired angle. Start at one corner of the framework and work outwards.*

3 *Secure the first board using decking screws. These are best screwed in using a power screwdriver. Prior to fastening it down, square off each end of this board so that it will lie flush with the frame.*

4 *Position the boards so that a straight edge can be placed on them and the angle at which each has to be cut can be marked with a pencil line. Ensure a small gap between each for subsequent fixing.*

Left: Well-constructed decking provides an ideal edge for a formal pool. Not only is it neat and pleasing to the eye, but it provides safe and easy access to the waterside for both pond maintenance and enjoyment. When installing decking, it is important to provide strong supports and to ensure that it is level in all directions. Only use purpose-made deckboards and ensure that they have been pressure-treated with a wood preservative that is harmless to fish and plant life.

5 *The gap between boards to allow for timber movement and surface drainage need only be minimal, but it should be uniform. The end of a carpenter's pencil can be utilized as a convenient unit of measure.*

6 *The boards are placed in position and secured with decking screws, at least two being used at each support point. It is important to ensure that they screw vertically into the timber for a secure fit.*

7 *There is usually a small carpentry task required at the end to ensure a neat finish. It is possible to run the decking out to an even number of boards, but this rarely produces ideal overall dimensions.*

using ready-made decking

In the past decking was often overwhelmingly linear in appearance. All the boards ran in the same direction, the only concessions being made at the corners where for strength, convenience and appearance right-angled joints were usually created.

However, with the increasing and widespread use of decking, especially in Europe and the USA, manufacturers and designers have appreciated that decking need not be simply functional, but can be an integral part of the designed landscape, making a major visual contribution to the outside living space. However, using just straight lengths of timber, the home gardener would have to be a reasonably skilled carpenter to achieve interesting patterns and variations that will have a powerful visual impact.

Realizing the limitations of the average home handyman, manufacturers have now come up with ready-made decking shapes in a series of appealing patterns and configurations. Squares of decking are the most popular, but hexagons, octagons, circles and other shapes are now freely available, many of which can be mixed and matched with one another. Elaborate features can be easily realized with modern decking squares.

While these can be used as part of traditional decking construction, they are also versatile enough to be attractively arranged to create landing stages and piers, the fixing arrangements being identical to those used for conventional decking construction, but with additional supports when several shapes are utilized together.

Left: Ready-made decking can be used to create wonderful design effects as well as to fulfil a function in the garden. It is very important when decking extends over the water that it has adequate support, especially when it is to be routinely used for recreational purposes, such as standing or sitting. Looking good is not enough, the structure must be safe as well.

USING DECKING SQUARES

1 *Measure and cut the support timbers so that they correspond exactly with the dimensions of the decking square.*

2 *Once cut to length, position the timbers in a square and check that the decking top fits exactly. Then screw the base together.*

3 *Provide central bearers to ensure that the platform is fully supported. Once the legs are secured, these will be screwed into position.*

5 *The whole framework can now be fastened together before the ready-made decking section is fitted on top of it.*

6 *The ready-made decking square is now ready for securing to the platform framework.*

4 *Using decking screws and a power screwdriver, fasten the boards that form the edge of the platform to the support legs.*

7 *Fasten the decking square using decking screws. It will fit snugly on the top of the support.*

When installed, ensure that the platform is level.

installing in-pool lighting

It is vital when installing lighting to have a very healthy respect for electricity, especially when it is in close proximity to water. Potentially this is a deadly combination. However, there should be no problem with in-pond lights providing that a reputable brand is purchased and all the instructions that are given with the equipment are adhered to properly.

Underwater lighting is quite safe – modern units are manufactured to operate with low-voltage cable and a transformer, and the light units themselves are specially sealed. For the best effect, underwater lighting can be placed beneath a fountain or waterfall feature to illuminate the tumbling water. Alternatively it can be situated at the edge of the pool pointing inwards to focus upon a particular ornament or plant grouping, or outwards to illuminate an object on the pond edge. The placement of lights is not an exact science and it may be necessary to reposition the lights several times before the desired effect is achieved.

This is where floating lights can come into their own. These function in exactly the same manner as static underwater lights but are more readily adjusted to suit prevailing conditions. Along with other electrical systems, it pays to think about what effects you want to create early in the planning stages of pond construction, so that not only can lighting positions be selected, but the necessary electrical connection points can be established close at hand. Floating candles are another 'low-tech' way of lighting a pond, but of course they are vulnerable to the prevailing weather conditions and likely to blow out on a windy night.

Some fountains have integral lights, which do not require any particular installation skills. However, it is important to position the fountain feature and pump on a secure flat plinth, and ideally in a position where the cable can be discreetly hidden as it enters the pond.

Above: *In-pool lighting can be most effective when used to highlight specific plants or pond ornaments. It is safe to use and available in a wide range of packages. Most have a transformer and white lights (right). However, the colour can be changed by clipping on a different lens. Some pond lighting kits have a mechanism for attaching them to a pump – this can rotate to give several timed colour changes.*

ATTACHING LIGHTS TO A FOUNTAIN

1 *One of the most effective lighting arrangements simply clips the spotlight to a pump beneath the fountain head.*

2 *The colour of the light can be changed by the use of differently coloured lenses which snap on to make a watertight seal.*

3 *The submersible pump and lights are placed into position in the pool. The lights point upwards beneath the fountain.*

4 *When switched on, the light should illuminate all the spray pattern. Slight adjustment of the lights may be necessary.*

Right: *An underwater spotlight need not be attached to a pump. Free-standing lights can also produce dramatic effects.*

installing external lights

The majority of exterior garden lights are installed after construction of the water feature is complete. Indeed it is often not until the pond is up and working that lighting is considered. It can then be tricky to achieve exactly the desired effect. It is better to regard lighting as an integral part of the project from the outset so that any mains cabling or weatherproof power sockets can be carefully incorporated into the original plan.

Water and electricity are not compatible in most situations, so it is important to use only purpose-designed outdoor lighting and to follow installation instructions to the letter. The majority of outdoor garden lighting systems operate from a transformer that is linked to the normal domestic electrical supply. The transformer reduces the voltage to a safe level which means that the low-voltage cables from the transformer to the light units can be run quite safely along the surface of the ground, or concealed amongst the surrounding plants.

This is particularly useful as it allows major adjustments to be made after the lights have been positioned and permits a certain amount of experimentation with the uplighting of various garden features and plants. No underground wiring is required unless the transformer is installed in a building away from the house. The lamps can be fitted anywhere along the cable by means of a simple screw connection and are completely portable.

Once the positioning of the lights has been determined, it may be considered desirable to bury the cable so that it does not catch on a hoe or fork while you are undertaking routine tasks. In this case use conduit to thread it through and install in a similar way to the method illustrated which is recommended for armoured cables.

MAKING IT SAFE

It is important with external lighting that every precaution is taken to guarantee safety. Waterproof connectors and plugs are essential, as is a system which uses a transformer to eliminate the risk of accidents. Follow the maker's instructions carefully.

SETTING UP EXTERNAL LIGHTS

1 *The modern garden lighting kit is safe and reliable. However, follow instructions at all times – don't be tempted to improvise.*

2 *A transformer ensures that the electrical power output into the garden is stepped down to a safe voltage.*

3 *When fixing the lights, determine the position you want them to be and then screw the connectors into the cable.*

4 *Any external cable carrying mains power should be of a waterproof armoured kind and laid in a conduit inside a trench.*

5 *Plastic cable conduits have snap-on covers that keep the wire safe from any disturbance by spade or fork.*

6 *Once the conduit is securely positioned in the foot of the trench, cover it over with a generous layer of builder's sand.*

7 *Cover the cable with tiles for additional protection. This is a sensible precaution to protect it from future disturbance.*

8 *Stretch electrical hazard tape along the run of tiles. This gives immediate warning of danger in case it should be unearthed*

9 *The individual lights are positioned discreetly at the poolside and focused upon carefully selected features in the pond.*

Above and right: *An entire water feature can be lit to give a dramatic appearance at night. Alternatively waterfalls, fountains or bridges can be selectively highlighted.*

making stepping stones

Although a wide range of stepping stones is available from garden centres these days, there is great satisfaction to be had from making your own. Not only is there an opportunity for originality, but stepping stones that are produced at home are generally cheaper and will fulfil the gardener's requirements exactly.

The style and shape of the stones is a matter of personal fancy, but size and weight do matter. The stones have to be able to be placed in position without too much man-handling and must be of a sufficient surface area safely to accommodate the larger foot and be of such a depth that they emerge above the surface of the water.

The easiest method of making stepping stones is to use concrete made with a fine pea gravel and to pour this into a mould. The mould can be of timber if the stones are to be rectangular, or of marine plywood if a more rounded shape is required. To create an interesting fluted or undulating edge, popular lawn edging materials can be cut to size and used in a box frame as illustrated to make a template for the stepping stone.

Make the stones on a flat surface. A wooden board or similar is ideal. Do not put the mould on a concrete slab or, once cast, the stepping stones will bond to the slab beneath. When using a timber mould it is important to soak it thoroughly or paint the inside of the mould with a mixture of garden lime and mortar to stop the concrete from sticking.

Stepping stones manufactured from concrete can be coloured by adding colorants at the wet mix stage and, before the concrete has set, interesting stippling or textured effects can be created on the surface of the stones.

CONCRETE MIX

The ideal concrete mixture comprises four parts by volume of aggregate, two parts concreting sand and one part cement. These are mixed together dry, water is added and the pile is mixed again.

MAKING A CIRCULAR STEPPING STONE

1 *Either purchase a ready-mixed dry concrete mixture or use gravel, sand and cement. Mix it all together until of a consistent grey colour. Add water gradually as mixing takes place. Do not permit the mixture to become sloppy.*

2 *The ideal mixture is of a consistent grey colour and sufficiently moist that when a shovel is moved back and forth in the heap, ridges are formed which retain their character and shape.*

3 *Make a small wooden frame to match the dimensions of the proposed stepping stone; you can create an interesting shape by using a piece of metal or plastic lawn edging.*

4 *Place the mould and frame on a piece of hardboard and then add the concrete mixture, making sure that all the indentations around the edge are filled.*

5 *Tamp the concrete so that moisture exudes. This also brings some of the sand and finer aggregate to the surface for a smoother finish. The concrete will set in two days and the stepping stone can be lifted out.*

Left: *Stepping stones provide a convenient means of crossing water, and they are also highly decorative. While natural stones can look appealing, manufactured stepping stones are often safer. They can also be more easily secured to a firm base.*

laying stepping stones

The installation of stepping stones requires some care. The positions selected should first of all be visually appealing. Stepping stones can be an intrusion rather than an asset in a water feature when poorly placed. Of course they must also be functional and easy to traverse, at the same time being secure and level.

Stepping stones are almost inevitably placed after construction has been completed and water added to the feature. In the case of a natural watercourse, it is difficult to assess their ideal position accurately with regard to depth unless water is flowing freely and at an average depth. However, this can create difficulties with installation, as stepping stones are ideally placed when the water is at its lowest level. The perfect solution with a naturally variable water course is to take average water depth measurements and then position the stepping stones at a time of minimal flow.

In an artificial situation this is not a problem. Water levels are either known, or if uncertain are tested, and then the stepping stones installed appropriately. The relationship of the surface of the stones to the level of the water can be easily assessed.

Whether the installation of stepping stones is in an artificial stream or pond, or for traversing a natural flow of water, stability is essential. The stones must be securely concreted or affixed to a level base and positioned sufficiently close to one another so that anyone crossing can do so with a normal gait. Take care to choose stones that have a naturally roughened surface – smooth surfaces are likely to become slippery when wet.

Below: Stepping stones are often principally for decoration. When used functionally, they must be placed at convenient even distances apart, ideally slightly closer than the length of an average stride.

5 *Secure each cross-piece with bolts in pre-drilled countersunk holes. It is imperative that all cross-members and supports align.*

6 *Drill the lengths of timber that are to form the walkway and secure them to the supports using substantial bolts.*

7 *Where there is a change in alignment of the causeway, make provision for the boards to fit neatly and evenly together.*

Above: *A causeway constructed from timber is an asset for both informal and formal water features. An offset arrangement of walkways like this breaks up the regularity of the construction, and encourages the walker to linger and admire the pool.*

installing an arched bridge

It is quite feasible to build an arched bridge from scratch, but it is more usual to purchase such a feature either ready-made or as a kit for self-assembly. When purchasing a kit or finished bridge, take care to ensure that all the dimensions are appropriate from both the practical and visual point of view. Also look carefully at the intended site before purchasing the bridge.

Even modest bridges are a considerable weight and must have sound foundations from both the point of view of safety and gradual settlement. If the soil slips, the bridge can twist and be damaged. So it is imperative that the positions of both ends of the bridge are thoroughly inspected and that suitable piers can be constructed to take the weight.

To be safe, the footings for each pier should be excavated to a depth of 60cm (2ft). Bridge piers can be pre-cast, but it can be simpler in most cases to cast them in position. For most bridges, digging holes of sufficient dimensions and filling them with concrete is adequate. Take care on clay soils which shrink badly and where appropriate include reinforcing rods in the piers.

When pre-cast piers are used then dig the holes at least 15cm (6in) larger all round than the piers themselves. Place them in position and pour in concrete. Alternatively you can build brick piers in the manner illustrated. Check that the piers on either bank are level and then install the bridge.

Right: *An arched bridge is an attractive focal point in many water gardens. The subtle curving form echoes the sinuous flow of water past the planted margins.*

7 *Cut holes in the hessian that are large enough to accommodate the small rootballs of young aquatic plants.*

8 *Push bare-rooted plants into the compost through the holes in the hessian and water thoroughly. Cut back any that are unstable.*

9 *Complete the planting arrangement using a combination of marginal and bog garden plants, both flowering and foliage subjects.*

PLANTING SUGGESTIONS

Plants Used

Acorus gramineus 'Variegatus'/summer/marginal
Alisma plantago-aquatica/summer/marginal
Calla palustris/summer/marginal
Carex pendula/summer/marginal
Carex riparia 'Variegata'/summer/marginal
Cyperus hybrid/summer/marginal
Mentha aquatica/summer/marginal
Osmunda regalis/fern
Primula pulverulenta/summer/bog

Alternative Plants

Acorus calamus 'Variegatus'/summer/marginal
Butomus umbellatus/summer/marginal
Caltha palustris/spring/marginal
Matteuccia struthiopteris/fern
Primula florindae/summer/bog
Veronica beccabunga/summer/marginal

Left: *It is important to anchor the island raft to the pond floor, or it will wander around the pool driven by the wind. Attach a rope with an anchoring weight. The rope should be the same length as the depth of water if the raft is to stay in one place.*

making a wet island

One of the easiest and most effective islands to create is one built of sandbags. Such is the versatility of these malleable shapes that it is possible to achieve quite sophisticated arrangements by grouping them together, as well as ones of formal design. Sandbags are readily available from builders' merchants and can be filled with either sand or soil as desired.

Using sand has the advantage of greater malleability and, although it is significantly heavier than soil, it does not contain nutrients which might escape into the water and create an algae problem. On the other hand the island is never going to become a real one from the plants' point of view, for roots are not going to penetrate the sand significantly and bind the island together. Indeed, a few years down the road, if not properly maintained with a

consistent level of water, the hessian may rot, the sand spill out and the island disintegrate.

Soil in the bags will be bound together by roots and become a solid island, but there are considerable hazards of the nutrients in the soil leaching out into the surrounding water. Even if the lower bags are filled with sub-soil or clay which is relatively inert, those in the upper layers where the plants are growing will be vulnerable to nutrient escape. However, algae and slimes will rapidly colonize the hessian and it will come to look quite natural.

The plants which will be established on sandbag islands will be bog or marginal subjects. A sandbag island is a wet island, the water table being at the level of the water in the pond which surrounds it, and so marginal and bog plants will thrive in this damp habitat.

MAKING A SANDBAG ISLAND

1 *Fill sandbags with river sand. Ensure that they are all of consistent size and shape.*

2 *Arrange the sandbags rather like bricks in alternate fashion to form a solid construction.*

3 *Complete the structure so that the sand bags at the top are just at final water level.*

4 *Fill the lower part of the island, where the plant roots are unlikely to penetrate, with hardcore.*

5 *Top up the central part of the island with suitable compost. Aquatic planting compost is the best medium to use.*

6 *Plant towards the edge of the island using trailing plants that will hang over the side and disguise the sandbags. Space these equally around the edge.*

7 *Fill the centre of the planting area with taller plants. Avoid invasive species which will crowd the centre.*

Above: *A wet island is most appropriate for an informal pond; whether man-made or naturally occurring, it is a pleasing addition.*

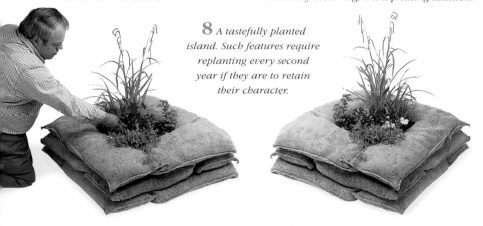

8 *A tastefully planted island. Such features require replanting every second year if they are to retain their character.*

PLANTING SUGGESTIONS

Plants Used

Carex pendula/summer/marginal
Cotula coronopifolia/summer/marginal
Lysimachia congestifolia 'Outback Sunset'/summer/bog
Mentha aquatica/summer/marginal
Mimulus x hybridus/summer/marginal
Preslia cervina/summer/marginal

Alternative Plants

Caltha palustris 'Flore Pleno'/spring/marginal
Houttuynia cordata/summer/marginal
Iris ensata/summer/bog
Iris sibirica/summer/bog
Lysimachia nummularia/summer/marginal

making a dry brick island

The simplest island to construct for the formal pool is one made of brick. Such construction need not be regimental and mathematical, although in practice it is easier to construct and visually most appealing if built in a square or rectangular shape. The other advantage of a brick island over any other form of construction is that it can be built as a dry island. That is one where the planting area within is drier than the marginal shelves or bog garden around the pond.

The bricks are laid in a conventional fashion to create a box-like effect, the lower layer being laid on fleece underlay positioned on top of the liner. When the island's position is known well in advance, a solid slab or foundation can be positioned beneath the pond liner as the feature is being built to provide a secure base.

A brick island has to be relatively tall to stand above the water and this quite naturally leaves a cavernous space within. However, it does not have to be totally filled with soil or compost, although many gardeners prefer to do so. The bottom half or third can consist of hardcore. If you want to make sure that the island is impermeable to seepage through the bricks, a membrane can then be placed on top of this and then brought up the sides as an inner liner.

In most cases the island can be left to its own devices, the water lapping to the top of the brickwork. However in the case of a dry island it is important that the top course of brickwork is above water level. This can often look ugly, in which case screw a plank of timber or a deck-board to the top layer of bricks. This produces a most attractive and quite natural finish.

BUILDING A BRICK ISLAND

1 *When a brick structure is built in a lined pool, it is a wise precaution to install a support slab beneath the liner.*

2 *Lay a generous bed of mortar for the first layer of bricks and ensure that they are both square and level.*

3 *The ends of the bricks must be 'buttered' with mortar to fill the gaps between them.*

4 *Lay the bricks in an alternate arrangement and ensure that each layer is level, square and vertical.*

5 *Once the mortar has dried thoroughly, a waterproofing sealant can be applied to the inner surfaces.*

6 *Fill the lower third of the structure with hardcore or gravel to provide drainage. Then top up with soil.*

LAYING STONES ON PLINTHS

1 *A generous mortar bed must be laid to enable a level brick base for each stepping stone to be constructed.*

2 *Start by positioning bricks in the corners. Ensure that these are set square. This base should be smaller than the stepping stone.*

3 *Continue to lay bricks, ensuring that each is laid on an even mortar bed and is separated from the next by a layer of mortar.*

4 *Continue construction with the joints of the bricks arranged in an alternate fashion. Check regularly to ensure that they are level.*

5 *A final layer of mortar is applied when the desired height has been reached in order to secure the stepping stone*

6 *Place the stepping stone gently into position on the mortar bed and firm into place. There should be a slight overhang.*

A stepping stone is rather like an iceberg, the majority of the structure being beneath the water. A strong construction of this kind is absolutely essential to ensure personal safety.

7 *Tap the stepping stone gently into position and make sure that it is level. Remove surplus mortar.*

making a wooden bridge

A wooden bridge or causeway provides an opportunity to see the water garden from another angle. Although they should be visually appealing, most wooden bridges are first and foremost functional. They are used rather than viewed.

Any bridge or causeway construction must have a secure foundation. This is not only necessary for the safe passage of people, but also ensures stability. Even a modest bridge can settle under its own weight if it is built with insufficient foundations. Ideally the bridge should be attached by bolts to concrete piers sunk into the ground to a depth of around 60cm (2ft). These are best cast in place and the bolts positioned in the concrete while it is still wet.

A causeway is really an extended bridge which takes the visitor across a large body of water, or alternatively criss-crosses a small water feature in an indirect fashion. Unlike a bridge where piers are created on either bank, a causeway is also attached to piers in the water.

The simplest method of creating supports for a causeway is to set short lengths of pipe into a concrete slab, or to bolt metal post supports to sturdy breeze blocks. The wooden supports for the bearers that will carry the planks of the causeway are dropped into these pipes after positioning in the pond. When such piers are created in a lined pool, it is important that they rest on a generous layer of fleece underlay to prevent damage to the liner.

In the creation of a wooden bridge or causeway, consider in which direction the timber planks lie. It is an established fact that if timbers are lying lengthways leading away from the bank, you are inclined to cross; if fastened crossways, you will probably linger on the bridge.

MAKING A WOODEN CAUSEWAY

1 *It is essential to have bolts firmly secured into the concrete basal supports.*

2 *Bolt the metal sleeves that will hold the bridge supports securely to the base.*

3 *Put the timber supports into the metal sleeves and make sure they are vertical.*

4 *Clamp a cross-member to each upright making sure that it is level. Use this as a template for the positioning of the other supports.*

Left: *The completed causeway – a neat and very economical method of bridging water attractively.*

7 *Choose suitable garden plants of varying flowering periods and plant as in the open garden. Here a shrub provides the focus.*

8 *A heavily planted dry island benefits from regular annual lifting and replanting.*

⸺ PLANTING SUGGESTIONS ⸺

Plants Used

Allium karataviense/summer/bulb
Armeria maritima var. lusitanica/
    summer/herbaceous
Genista lydia/spring/shrub
Saxifraga umbrosa/spring/herbaceous

Alternative Plants

Allium 'Purple Sensation'/summer/bulb
Alyssum saxatile/spring/herbaceous
Cytisus kewensis/spring/shrub
Dianthus 'Doris'/summer/herbaceous

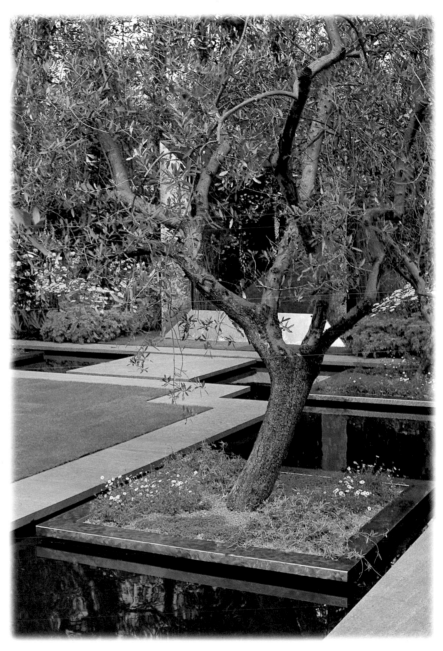

Above: *A dry island enables plants that are not usually associated with water to be employed in creating imaginative designs.*

Even sizeable garden trees can be included provided that they do not have root systems which will damage the island structure.

49

edging with paving stones

Edging with stones, slabs and bricks looks most effective around a formal pond. Such edging can be applied to informal ponds, but it is much more difficult to create a convincing effect. With square, rectangular and circular ponds, however, it is very attractive.

As with most other aspects of construction, it is sensible to work out the requirements for all the elements from the beginning. There is nothing more irritating than to construct a pond, only to find when the paving comes to be laid that one slab has to be cut on each side in order to finish the edging evenly, when a simple measurement before the excavation of the pond began would have resolved the problem.

Levels are also important. The pool should be level from side to side and end to end, the surrounding land having also been levelled in order to accommodate the paving. When laid, the slabs or bricks should also be level from side to side and end to end if the finished result is to be both functional and be satisfying visually. Remember to leave sufficient width of liner around the margins of the pool so that the paving stones can anchor the liner securely. It is a good idea to allow for a small overhang over the edge of the pool to disguise the point where the liner overlaps the surrounding soil.

With stones, pavers and bricks, safety is very important. A loose slab can tip an unwary visitor into the pond, so sufficient mortar of suitable strength must be used to ensure that the slabs or bricks are bedded down securely. There are also dangers with mortar of polluting the water, as escaping lime or cement can cause eye irritation in fish. So work carefully and consider using small strips of cardboard or wood as shuttering to prevent the cement used either as the foundation or as pointing from slipping into the pool until it dries and becomes hard.

PAVING PATTERNS

Basket Weave *One of the simplest layouts and very effective when paving of a single colour is used. For a more dramatic effect, use pavers of two different colours.*

90° Herringbone *An arrangement which can be used for formal edging situations. It can look very effective with contrasting coloured paving stones set around it.*

45° Herringbone *A quite complex arrangement which is best executed in paving stones of contrasting colours. It is difficult to accommodate to a pool edge.*

Left: A formal pond is clearly defined by a paving stone edging. It is simple to create a straight edge for a square pond, but a circular one needs a little more inventiveness or the purchase of paving stones which have curved edges. These are now quite readily available.

EDGING A POOL WITH PAVERS

1 Lay a generous even bed of mortar close to the edge of the pool for securing the paving.

2 Lay the paving stones on the mortar bed with a slight overhang. This neatens the edge.

3 The second row of paving stones can be used to secure the edge of the liner in position.

4 Cut off any surplus liner and firm the second row of paving securely on the mortar bed.

5 Brush a dry mortar mix into the joints between the paving stones taking care not to let any drop into the pond. Water gently to ensure that it will set properly.

6 When the edge is complete, wash off any mortar splashes. Tie the water feature to the garden landscape by using cobbles or laying turf up to the paving stone edging.

edging with a cobble beach

With the popularity of wildlife ponds, the cobble beach has come into its own. It is not only seen as a method of edging the pond attractively, but also as providing a ready access for wildlife, especially birds, to enjoy the watery world. It also serves as an exit for small animals which might fall into the pond, but which can then clamber to safety.

An effective method of constructing a beach is firstly to excavate a shallow, sloping incline at one of the margins of the pond. The liner should be stretched over this area and then secured, either by lifting the surrounding soil or turf and tucking the liner underneath, or by trapping it between two rows of bricks or stones. If the beach is not just for birds and is going to take some pressure from foot traffic, then a shallow concrete footing can be made to trap the liner. This should be continuous for the length of the beach and immovable.

Where bricks are being used, the liner should be pulled tight and secured. The area in front and behind the bricks or footing can then be covered with cobbles to create an informal look, and this arrangement of stones then extended to the water's edge. Of all the methods of edging, the beach is the cheapest and also one of the most appealing, but remember that it is not suitable for heavy foot traffic.

While cobbles are the easiest objects to use to create a beach which looks natural, there are many other materials that can be used in their place. Shells, both natural and coloured, along with smoothed coloured glass chips or marbles can also be successfully used. Even sharp sand can be employed. However, although this looks good at first, it does tend to grow a film of algae and requires constant disturbance by brushing or raking if it is to retain its attractiveness.

Above: *A cobble and slate beach is a very neat way of finishing the edge of an informal pond. Carefully constructed, it provides easy access for wildlife to drink and bathe, and is also home to all sorts of aquatic insect life.*

CREATING A COBBLE BEACH

1 *Secure the liner with turf or an edge of bricks. This is essential and provides a solid base upon which the beach is constructed.*

2 *It is generally advisable to lay at least two rows of bricks or stones. The liner can be trapped in place between them*

3 *Once the mortar has set, cobbles can be added, the larger ones being positioned first and covering the bricks.*

4 *A mixture of well-washed pebbles and cobbles can then be added and heaped up to depth of 15 to 20cm (6-8in).*

5 *To prevent cobbles rolling into the bottom of the pool create a barrier using larger stones. These will be totally submerged.*

Above: *A cobble beach provides a natural and easily maintained transition from lawn to pond. It is not only practical and easy to maintain but visually very appealing.*

edging with timber

Timber is not as permanent a solution to edging a pond as paving, but it does have its uses. When a pond is being constructed in conjunction with timber decking, then timber edging is a natural extension of the feature. It is also a good way of completing raised pools of timber construction, such as those made from railway sleepers and liner. It also looks appropriate in rustic settings, even though the wood is prepared and treated formally.

There are a number of ways of fixing timber, these depending upon the visual effect that it is desired. When the surface of the soil is to be level with the surrounding ground, then an innovative system must be employed with a specially constructed concrete surround being built into which the timber can be bolted. The liner is trapped between this timber and wooden edging that will rest just in the water. Timber plating joints are used to hold the two wooden sections tightly together. Their screws do not penetrate the liner and allow the water to come right to the top without seepage.

A similar system can be used with timber replacing the traditional concrete component. It will not be quite as long-lived, but will last sufficiently for most gardeners. Here it is important to use good long screws, those recommended for decking being ideal. Providing that the timber edging is well treated with preservative it will make a durable and fine-looking edging.

Apart from the horizontal use of timber edging, the upright log-roll type material so frequently used for creating and edging flower beds can also be pressed into use using similar methods of fixing.

USING TIMBER

The use of timber as an edging is ideal for the do-it-yourself enthusiast. Modern timbers for garden use are now widely available already treated with a preservative. It is important for a high quality finish to use good tools and to measure accurately.

MAKING A TIMBER SURROUND

1 *A raised wooden pond can be successfully edged with timber, but protective underlay is advisable to prevent the liner from rubbing.*

2 *Pull the liner tightly over the pool edge smoothing out the wrinkles and creating bold folds of liner to take up the slack.*

3 *Screw the timber edging securely to the pool framework. It is advisable to use decking screws as these are rustproof.*

Above: *Timber is one of the most versatile, natural and attractive edging materials for the garden pond.*

4 *Cut off the surplus liner. Allow for a small overhang so that the final trimming of the liner can be concealed beneath this.*

5 *There are many attractive wood stains and preservatives available which are quite safe to use in close proximity to water.*

6 *The finished timber edge not only secures the pond liner, but becomes an important element of the visual structure.*

using natural grass edging

Right: Grass is one of the most attractive pond edgings, but it is very maintenance intensive.

Grass can be a most effective natural edging and, although it does present a few minor maintenance problems, it is well worth considering in a natural setting. The important consideration with a traditional turf edging is the depth of soil required up to the edge of the pond to maintain the health of the grass.

To ensure that grass edging does not dry out, it is necessary to have a minimum depth of 5cm (2in) of soil, although 10cm (4in) is preferable. There is nothing worse than a bright green summer lawn rolling out to a water garden where the grass immediately adjacent the pool edge is yellow or parched through lack of moisture.

If the edge is carefully arranged and the grass laid as turf, then this can be put in contact with the water which by capillary action spreads up and through the sward. It will

soak up quite an amount of water during hot summer weather and so care will be needed to ensure that the pool is regularly topped up to maintain the required water level to keep the grass healthy. Where this is successful, another problem sometimes follows: vigorous uncontrolled growth, especially of grass roots that dangle down into the pond all around the margins.

This can be overcome by using a specially selected turf that will grow and prosper on rockwool. This is an inert material widely used for soil-less plant culture, and when used as a pool edging it is neat, clean cut and very successful in containing the spread of root growth. While horticultural rockwool of a high quality is to be preferred, household rockwool used by the building industry for roof insulation has proved to be quite satisfactory also.

TURF AND ROCKWOOL EDGING

Right: Grass is a pleasing edging medium for a water garden, but it rapidly grows out of control and creates maintenance problems by invading the margins.

1 *The use of good quality turf, especially of non-rhizomatous grasses, along with rockwool can ensure a permanently tidy edge to the pond.*

2 *Lift and remove the matted roots of overgrown turf. Cut back to 30cm (12in) beyond the edge.*

3 *Excavate so that a section of rockwool of the dimensions of the turf can be inserted.*

4 *Ensure that the new turf can be laid on the rockwool and then water it thoroughly.*

5 *Lay the new turf on the dampened rockwool ensuring a neat edge at the poolside.*

6 *Water the turf thoroughly. You must do this regularly until the turf and rockwool knit together. This usually takes a month or more. An occasional weak liquid feed is invaluable.*

7 *The rockwool will act as a sponge if in contact with the water. When the turf does not touch the water, weekly watering of the edge is advisable to maintain an attractive green sward.*

edging with coir roll

For pools that are informal and are required to take on a natural appearance, the use of coir rolls which are planted up with marginal aquatics can be recommended. Coir is a by-product of the coconut industry and is a very fibrous material with few nutrients which is ideal for plant root development and growth. By virtue of its shortage of nutrients, there is no danger of organic material leaching into the pool which would encourage the development of algae in the water. On the contrary the coir will tend to take up nutrients as it starts slowly to decompose; the plants will also absorb their fair share and so benefit the underwater eco-system.

Coir rolls are common in the landscape industry, coir being packed into large sausage-shaped packets wrapped with coarse rope-work or hessian. On a smaller scale gardeners can recreate the same or a similar effect utilizing hessian sandbags or old tights. Indeed the rolls can be made so that they fit on to the marginal shelves exactly, coir compost from the garden centre then being used as the filling.

Plants are planted through small slits made in the hessian and, if kept well watered, they will quickly establish. In spring or summer rolls can be placed out on the marginal shelves either pre-planted or ready for planting. Try to keep compatible varieties of marginal aquatics in the same bag using those that grow at similar rates to prevent the swamping of one variety by another. Once established with the planted roll pushed hard against the back of the marginal shelf, there will be a seamless transition from pool to garden, the plants leading the eye unerringly from land to water. Coir also has the benefit of not disturbing the pond's eco-system.

PLANTING A COIR ROLL

3 *Once the roll has been filled, check that it is of the correct dimensions for its intended position. Tie up the open end and then cut small planting holes into it at suitable intervals.*

1 *Using hessian or a sandbag stitch and create a long sausage-like roll. This should be of a size which can be conveniently handled and will rest easily on the margin or against the pond edge.*

2 *Fill the hessian roll with finely milled coir. Unlike other organic composts, coir – a by-product of the coconut industry – contributes little to the nutrient balance and eco-system of the pond.*

4 *Use a range of non-invasive marginal plants, such as aquatic irises, for planting. Insert these bare-rooted through the holes.*

5 *Only include plants which grow at more or less the same rate.*

···· PLANTING SUGGESTIONS ····

Plants Used

Carex pendula/summer/marginal
Carex riparia 'Variegata'/summer/marginal
Iris ensata 'Variegata'/summer/bog
Mentha aquatica/summer/marginal
Mimulus cardinalis/summer/bog

Alternative Plants

Butomus umbellatus/summer/marginal
Caltha palustris/spring/marginal
Iris laevigata/summer/marginal
Preslia cervina/summer/marginal
Veronica beccabunga/summer/marginal

Right: *A coir roll in which primulas have become established. The roll is hidden and the union of pond and garden is seamless.*

maintaining the eco-balance

A water feature is only successful if the eco-system is in balance. There are exceptions with very small pools or fast-moving water where a natural balance of any kind is impossible to achieve, but most water features should be able to settle into a pattern of self-sustainable balance.

Where this is not practical, then chemical means usually have to be employed in order to retain water sweetness and clarity. Sometimes merely changing water will serve the purpose, but this is often difficult to undertake regularly and is usually very time-consuming.

The principles behind creating a natural balance are very clear. Submerged plants mop up nutrients in the water and provide daytime oxygen for fish and other submerged creatures. They are also coincidentally a food source for some fish and other aquatic inhabitants. By removing excess nutrients they make life difficult for the single-celled algae which otherwise turn the water green and produce a pea-soup effect. Generally the more submerged aquatics there are the better, but there should be at least ten bunches planted for each square metre (c.11sq ft) of surface area of open water.

The presence of algae is also influenced by the amount of sunlight falling beneath the water. For submerged plants such light is vital, but it need not illuminate all the watery depths. At least a third of the surface area should be shaded by floating aquatics or the leaves of waterlilies and other deep-water aquatics. Other forms of shade, such as that cast by a building or trees are not quite the same and bring their own problems, particularly general poor growth of other aquatics as well as those of leaf accumulation when trees are used.

Marginal aquatics brighten up the water feature, but make little difference to the water garden eco-system. Where the foliage or flowers are especially attractive to wildlife, then this is an added bonus. Likewise fish are useful in that they control aquatic insect pests, but for the most part they are purely decorative and should be introduced sparingly.

Moving water can also be embraced by a balanced eco-system, but the introduction of floating plants is not practical when water is flowing, and the establishment of waterlilies and several other deep-water aquatic species is difficult as they resent moving water, so providing shade to the surface of the water is not so easy. However, the introduction of simple natural or biological filtration can resolve this problem another way.

POND MAINTENANCE

Above: It is important to remove algae regularly. On cobbled beaches, the only successful method of control is by hand.

Below: Aquatic snail species with pointed shells cause damage to water plants. They should be caught and removed, if possible.

Above: Submerged plants are necessary to ensure a good eco-balance in a pool. They must be thinned if they grow too profusely.

Below: *With the careful use of submerged aquatics and both floating and deep-water plants, a naturally sustaining balance can be successfully achieved.*

seasonal care

The spring is the best time for establishing plants and introducing fish to a pond or water feature. There are one or two very early flowering aquatic species, notably amongst the marsh marigolds, and these are best planted immediately flowering is over unless established in a container. When spring planting is not possible, then summer establishment can be undertaken. All aquatic plants happily transplant at that time, but often have to be cut back in order to establish properly, thereby ruining their period of floral beauty for that season.

Spring is traditionally propagation time, and apart from conventional division, waterlilies can be increased from 'eyes' and water forget-me-nots and mimulus from seed. The cuttings of plants like brooklime and watermint are best rooted during early summer when the flush of early growth subsides.

Fish can be introduced to the pond at any time during spring or summer. When introducing new fish it is a wise precaution to dip them in methylene blue to disinfect them against maladies such as fungus and fin rot. These

CLEANING LIGHTS

Right: *Periodically underwater lights require removing from the pond and cleaning. They are of a shape which seems to attract blanket weed and silkweed to cling to them. In order to ensure the best quality light, the lenses require regular attention. A stiff brush is the best way of returning them to a pristine condition.*

Left: *To maintain this attractive pond in good order requires regular care. Attention for half an hour each week will keep it looking good all year round. Topping up with water to compensate for evaporation must be undertaken regularly.*

Above and above right: Although one of the most attractive floating plants, fairy moss (Azolla caroliniana) *can get out of control and smother other plants. Removal with a net is the only solution.*

diseases spread quickly, especially in a well balanced pond where there are healthy fish. Never place new introductions into a pond until disinfection has taken place or you risk the health of your existing stock.

During the summer it is very much a matter of keeping on top of blanket weed whenever it appears, twisting it out with a stick. Aquatic plants should be regularly manicured, fading blossoms and foliage being removed and when necessary dense floating subjects, such as fairy moss, rationalized. Submerged plants can be thinned, but very cautiously as removing too many will disrupt the natural balance of the pond.

As autumn arrives the pump should be removed, cleaned and put into store to be replaced by a pool heater. The same goes for other submerged equipment, such as in-pool lights and fountain heads. Net the pond or its surrounds to prevent leaves accumulating in the water as when they decompose they produce noxious gases which in an ice-covered pond are dangerous for fish. Never transplant aquatic plants in the autumn, it is only true bog plants that can be moved safely in their dormant state. Autumn is a good time to scrub surfaces that are walked on, such as decks, bridges, stepping stones and pond

edges, to remove any accumulated slime that might make them slippery and unsafe.

Winter care of a water feature is minimal. If water freezes over and there are fish present, then ensure that the ice is vented to allow for the exchange of air. Do not hit the ice to break it – this creates shock waves that can concuss the fish. Instead, boil some water in a pan, then stand the hot pan on the ice and allow it to melt through. This creates a hole in the ice through which gases can permeate. All popular aquatic plants are completely hardy and will come to no harm during winter.

Above: At the approach of winter and again in spring, it is important to scrub decking in order to remove encrusted algae and other debris. A stiff brush and soapy water is an effective treatment.

index

Picture Credits

Eric Crichton Photos: 3 (design: Mark Davis, RHS Hampton Court 2001), 4 (Mrs Una Carr, (NGS) Avon), 8-9 (design: S. Rendell & J. Tavender, Dorset Water Lily Co, RHS Hampton Court 2001), 9 (RHS Chelsea 1997), 12-13 (Wyevale Garden Centres, RHS Chelsea 1997), 18 (Mitsubishi Garden, RHS Hampton Court 2001), 20 (design: Mamey Hall, RHS Hampton Court 2001), 21 left, 24-25 (design: Crockett and Summers, Dorset Water Lily Co, RHS Hampton Court 1999), 26 (design: Charles Funk, Evening Standard, RHS Chelsea 2001), 29 (as 8-9), 37 (The Quarryman Garden, RHS Chelsea 1998), 49 (design: Arabella Lennox-Boyd, Evening Standard, RHS Chelsea 2000), 51 ('Country Living', RHS Chelsea 1993), 55, 59, 61 (design: Daniel Lloyd-Morgan, Anglo Aquarium Plant Co, RHS Hampton Court 2001). **John Glover:** 13 bottom, 16-17, 17 top, 25 top, 47. **Jerry Harpur:** 6 (Villa Bebek Bali), 13 top (design: David Stevens, RHS Chelsea 1993), 23 (Susanna Brown and Catalyst TV). **Marcus Harpur:** 11 left (London Borough of Barnet, RHS Chelsea 2001), 52 (Paul Dyer, RHS Hampton Court 2001). **S. and O. Mathews:** 18-19, 21 right, 38. **Clive Nichols Garden Pictures:** 7 (Leyhill Prison, RHS Chelsea 2000), 10 (Garden & Security Lighting), 11 right (Garden & Security Lighting), 14, 22, 25 bottom (Brook Cottage, Oxon), 27 (design: Ann Firth), 33 (Garden & Security Lighting), 35 (Garden & Security Lighting), 41 (Architectural Plants, Sussex), 42 (Little Coopers, Hampshire), 57 (Mr Fraser/design: Julian Treyer-Evans), 62 (Vale End, Surrey). **Neil Sutherland:** 1, 5, 8, 15, 17 bottom, 19, 30.